I0878797

DRAGON FIELD GUIDES

DRAGONS among Us

A Field Guide

TAYLOR FENMORE

Lerner Publications ◆ Minneapolis

Copyright © 2026 by Lerner Publishing Group, Inc.

All rights reserved. International copyright secured. No part of this book may be reproduced, stored in a retrieval system, or transmitted in any form or by any means—electronic, mechanical, photocopying, recording, or otherwise—without the prior written permission of Lerner Publishing Group, Inc., except for the inclusion of brief quotations in an acknowledged review.

Lerner Publications Company
An imprint of Lerner Publishing Group, Inc.
241 First Avenue North
Minneapolis, MN 55401 USA

For reading levels and more information, look up this title at www.lernerbooks.com.

Main body text set in Aptifer Sans LT Pro.
Typeface provided by Linotype AG.

Editor: Angel Kidd **Designer:** Athena Currier **Photo Editor:** Angel Kidd
Lerner team: Martha Kranes

Library of Congress Cataloging-in-Publication Data

Names: Fenmore, Taylor, author.
Title: Dragons among us : a field guide / Taylor Fenmore.
Description: Minneapolis, MN : Lerner Publications, [2025] | Series: Dragon field guides | Includes bibliographical references and index. | Audience: Ages 8–11. | Audience: Grades 4–6. | Summary: "Many real-life animals look and act a lot like dragons! From flying lizards and spiky snakes to frilled fish and horned caterpillars, readers will discover awesome creatures with dragon-like features"— Provided by publisher.
Identifiers: LCCN 2024043499 (print) | LCCN 2024043500 (ebook) | ISBN 9798765669334 (library binding) | ISBN 9798765683989 (paperback) | ISBN 9798765677056 (epub)
Subjects: LCSH: Morphology (Animals)—Juvenile literature. | Dragons—Juvenile literature.
Classification: LCC QL799.3 .F46 2025 (print) | LCC QL799.3 (ebook) | DDC 597.95/5—dc23/eng/20241119

LC record available at https://lccn.loc.gov/2024043499
LC ebook record available at https://lccn.loc.gov/2024043500

Manufactured in the United States of America
1-1011749-53904-2/5/2025

Table of Contents

Waiting for Dinner

A dragon moray eel peeks between the ridges of a coral reef. Its long, snakelike body helps it move easily through gaps in the reef. Its orange and brown scales with white and black spots help it blend in with its surroundings. Smaller fish and other prey have a hard time seeing it.

The eel waits for a smaller fish to swim by. Then it sneaks out. It snatches the fish with its sharp teeth.

The dragon moray eel is similar to a dragon. With its pointed teeth and snakelike body, it looks similar to some dragons. The way it waits in a reef to find food is similar to how some dragons wait in caves or forests for prey to come near them.

A dragon moray eel waits for prey on a reef.

Dragons are not real. But like the dragon moray eel, there are many animals that look or act like dragons from stories. Can you think of any animals that remind you of a dragon?

CHAPTER 1

Lots of Lizards

Like most dragons, lizards are reptiles. That might be why dozens of lizard species look similar to dragons. Most lizards have four legs, tough scales, and long tails. Some have special spines or crests on their bodies. Some lizards even act like dragons.

Komodo Dragon

Some people say the Komodo dragon might be the closest animal to a real-life dragon. Komodo dragons are the biggest lizard species in the world. They have tough scales that cover

Komodo dragons live on five islands in Indonesia.

their bodies and long tails. They also produce venom as some dragons do. Many dragons prefer to be alone. Komodo dragons are solitary too. Both creatures might attack another lizard or other animal that enters their space.

LARGE LIZARDS

The largest Komodo dragon was 10.3 feet (3.1 m) long and weighed 366 pounds (166 kg).

Special Spines and Scales

Many dragons have special physical features. Detailed crests might surround a dragon's head. Or extra-tough scales or ridges might go down its back.

Many lizard species have similar features. Bearded dragons have showy spikes around their face. Much like a dragon's crest, these spikes surround their head.

Water dragons don't have crests. Instead, they have a ridge of spikes on the back of their head. Thinner, shorter spikes trail down their back and tail.

The armadillo lizard has special scales. Their scales are broad and tough. Each one ends in a spike. These lizards' spikes and wide mouth remind many people of dragons.

Armadillo lizards defend themselves by curling into a ball and showing their spiky scales.

Cool Crest

The frilled lizard has a wide frill around its neck. The frill often lays flat. But when a frilled lizard is scared or angry, it raises the frill and runs on its two back legs. At rest, the frill looks similar to the crests that some dragons have. When it expands, it even looks like a dragon's wings.

Frilled lizards expand their frills to look bigger and scarier.

A gliding Draco lizard

Flying Lizards

Most dragons can fly. Some fly with wings. Others glide or float through the air.

Draco lizards can fly too. Often called flying lizards, these animals have a thin, scaly sheet of skin between their front and back legs. When they jump from tall places such as trees, this skin allows them to glide on air.

CHAPTER 2
Snake or Dragon?

Snakes are reptiles with long tails, wide mouths, and usually slitted pupils. They look a lot like wingless dragons, such as the long of China and Vietnam, as well as the Rainbow Serpents of West Africa and Australia. Some snakes have unique features that make them extra dragonlike.

Spiked and Spined

Like lizards, some snakes have special spines or spiky scales that remind people of dragons. The dragon snake is one of these species. At first glance, it might seem plain. It has small, black scales and a wide, flat head. But the dragon snake isn't smooth like many other snake species. Its scales are rough. And it has two special ridges running side by side down its body, similar to the ridges on some dragons' backs.

Dragon snakes can grow up to 2.5 feet (.8 m) long.

Hairy bush vipers are sometimes called spiny bush vipers.

The hairy bush viper is another snake with rough scales. But it doesn't have ridges like the dragon snake. Instead, this snake's scales flair out in sharp points. The spiked scales on its head look a lot like a dragon's crest.

The dragon snake and hairy bush viper sometimes act like dragons too. Many dragons live on their own. These snake species also keep to themselves.

FACT VS. FICTION

Dragons would look more like lizards than snakes.

FICTION!

There are many kinds of dragons. Some look a lot like lizards, with four legs and crests around their heads. Others are more like snakes, with long bodies and no legs. But some dragons have traits of both animals. And others don't look like either a snake or a lizard at all. If dragons were real, there would probably be a mix of lizardlike and snakelike ones.

In South Korea, dragons are called yong.

Green anacondas can swim up to 10 miles (16 km) per hour.

Pterodactyl fossil skeleton

DRAGON OR DINOSAUR?

When people first found the fossils of dinosaurs, some believed the bones were from dragons. Dinosaur bones helped spread dragon myths.

The Biggest Snake

Most dragons are very big. They are taller or longer than the average human. The anaconda is longer than most humans too. In fact, anacondas are the largest snakes in the world. Their giant size and slow slither remind some people of dragons. Anacondas can grow up to 30 feet (9.1 m) long and weigh up to 550 pounds (250 kg). The average human is between 5 to 6 feet (1.5 to 1.8 m) tall.

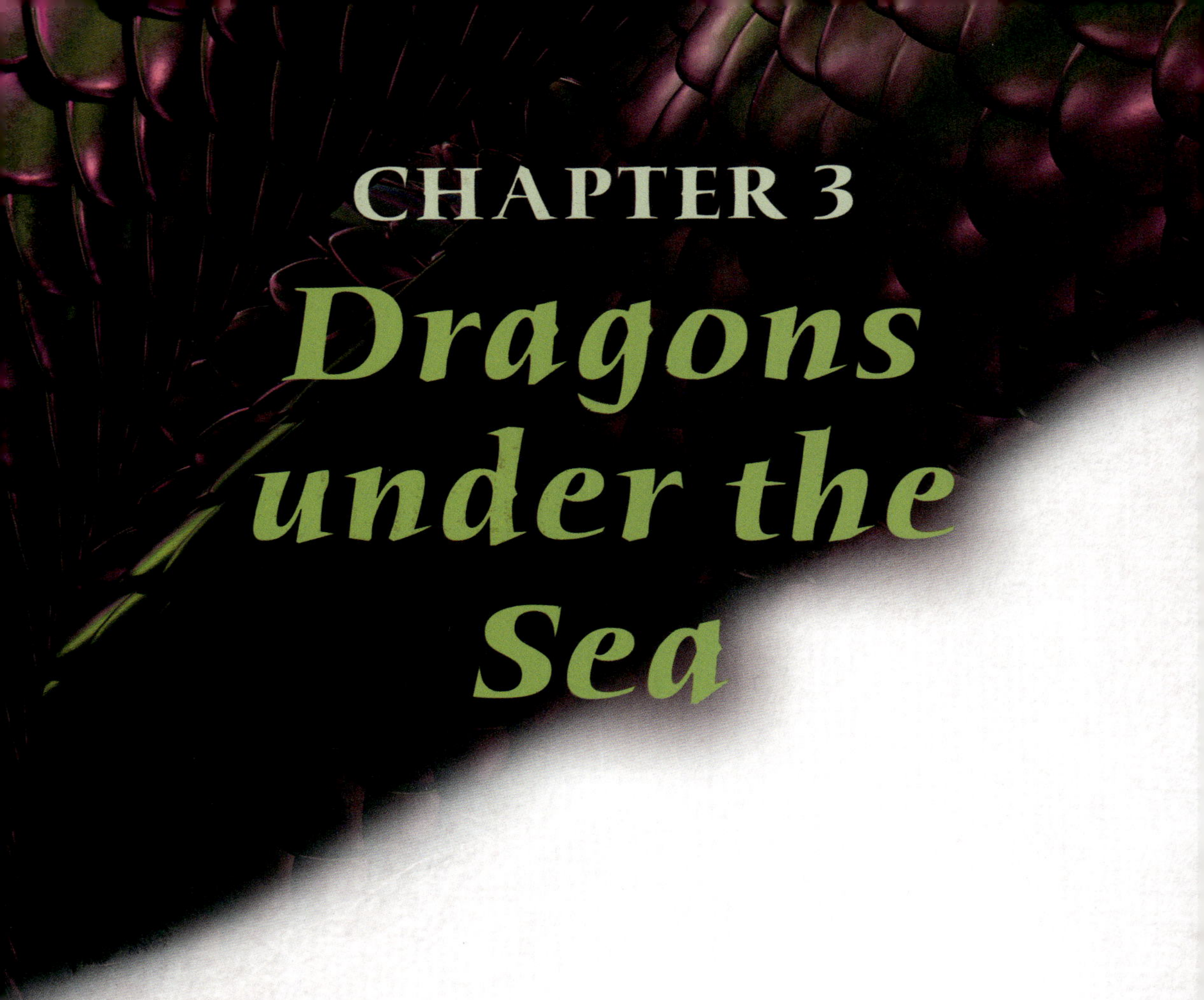

CHAPTER 3

Dragons under the Sea

Many lizards and snakes seem like dragons come to life. But many other animals have dragonlike traits too. Have you ever gone looking for a dragon underwater?

Fantastic Frills

Some dragons, such as the Korean yong, have detailed crests around their head. They may also have fans at the ends of their tail. The leafy sea dragon and the blue dragon sea slug have detailed frills and fins too.

Leafy sea dragons blend in with seagrass and surprise prey.

The leafy sea dragon is a fish that lives in rocky reefs and seagrass. Its many fins and frilled limbs look like leaves. And it has a long, tubelike mouth that is similar to a dragon's snout. A leafy sea dragon hunts like some dragons from stories too. It waits for prey, such as shrimp, to swim close. Then it sucks up the prey to eat.

This blue dragon sea slug is only 1.2 inches (3 cm) long.

The blue dragon sea slug has six limbs. Each limb has several tendrils, or long, thin body parts. They spread like wings as the sea slug moves. Sometimes it looks like the slug is flying through the water.

Slim and Slimy

Like snakes, some sea animals look like wingless dragons. The dragon moray eel has a long, slim body. Sharp teeth line its curved jaw. They do not make venom, but some moray eels are toxic. They have a slimy outer layer on their skin that can harm people or animals.

Olms look a lot like the Chinese long, the Korean yong, and other Asian dragons. They have long bodies with four short limbs. Their flat heads are wider than their bodies.

LONG LIVE THE OLM

Dragons can live for hundreds or thousands of years. Olms (*below*) don't live that long. But they do live about seventy years!

Olms have frilled gills near the back of their head that look like a dragon's crest. These gills help an olm sense what is around it.

Chinese long have crests much like olms and axolotls.

Axolotls breathe underwater as some dragons do.

Axolotls are similar to olms—and dragons! They have four short limbs and a wide, flat head. They also have three crestlike horns on each side of their head. These are an axolotl's gills. They look like frills or feathers, much like some dragon crests.

CHAPTER 4

More Dragon Look-alikes

All sorts of animals have dragonlike features. Animals with scales such as lizards, snakes, and some fish might come to mind first. But can you think of a bug that looks like a dragon? What about a bird?

Dragonlike Bugs

Several bugs make people think of dragons. For example, the dragon-headed caterpillar is named for its looks. This caterpillar has a flat head with four horns. Some dragons have horns that look similar to this insect's. Dragon-headed caterpillars share another trait with dragons too. Some species of this caterpillar make venom. They can sting other animals with their venom.

The pink dragon millipede gets its name from its shape and spines. It has a long, slim body like many wingless dragons. Pink spines cover its body. These spines look like the ridges some dragons have. But pink dragon millipedes have a lot more of them.

A pink dragon millipede

HUNDREDS OF CATERPILLARS

The dragon-headed caterpillar (*below*) is not a species of its own. About four hundred species of butterflies start their lives as this type of caterpillar.

Fancy Feathers

Many birds have dragonlike features too. The great eared nightjar is one. These birds are known for their dragonlike head. They have a short face and can open their beak very wide. The feathers on top of their head gather into a point on each side. It makes them look like they have horns, just as some dragons do.

Great eared nightjars live in forests in southeast Asia.

Even More Real-life Dragons

Animals all around the world remind people of dragons. Scaly reptiles, frilled fish, strange bugs, horned birds, and more share physical features with dragons from stories. Some animals act like dragons too. They might hunt or eat like a dragon. Or they might move like a dragon or make venom like one.

Have you ever seen an animal that reminds you of a dragon? What did it look like? What was it doing? Talk about it with a friend. You might come up with even more animals that remind you of dragons.

A Look at Wyrms

Some wyrms have horns or crests.

Wyrms are snakelike dragons. Like serpents, they have large heads with slitted eyes and long bodies. Some have wings, and others don't. Most do not have legs. If they do, their legs are very short. Some of these dragons live in water, such as oceans or deep pools. Others might travel underground. A wyrm that travels underground uses its head like a shovel to make a path. Wyrms can be dangerous. They slither quickly. Some have venom. Others breathe fire.

Glossary

crest: a showy growth of skin, fur, or feathers on or around the head of an animal

fossil: the remains of a plant or animal preserved in earth or rock

gill: an organ that fish and some other water-dwelling animals use to breathe underwater

limb: any of the paired parts of an animal that stick out from the body and are used mostly in moving or grasping, such as an arm or a leg

prey: an animal hunted or killed by another animal for food

reptile: a cold-blooded animal that lays eggs and is often covered with scales or other hard body parts

solitary: living or being alone

species: a group of living things that are related and produce offspring

venom: poison produced by some animals and passed to others, usually by biting or stinging

Learn More

Britannica Kids: Dragon
https://kids.britannica.com/kids/article/dragon/353064

Clarke, Ginjer L. *Are Dragons Real?* New York: Penguin Young Readers, 2021.

Kaiser, Brianna. *Dragon Anatomy: A Field Guide*. Minneapolis: Lerner Publications, 2026.

Kiddle: Leafy Sea Dragon Facts for Kids
https://kids.kiddle.co/Leafy_seadragon

Macfarlane, Tamara. *Dragon World*. New York: DK, 2021.

National Geographic Kids: Anaconda
https://kids.nationalgeographic.com/animals/reptiles/facts/anaconda

Index

Photo Acknowledgments

Image credits: d3_plus D.Naruse @ Japan/Getty Images, p. 5; USO/Getty Images, p. 7; hennymartina/Getty Images, p. 8; reptiles4all/Getty Images, p. 9; Ken Griffiths/Getty Images, p. 10; Nature Picture Library/Alamy, pp. 11, 14; gerraldkevin/Shutterstock, p. 13; Andrew Michael/Alamy, p. 15; Julian Gunther/Getty Images, p. 16; Corbin17/Alamy, p. 17; barbaraaaa/Getty Images, p. 19; Oxford Scientific/Getty Images, p. 20; Pavel Dudek/Alamy, p. 21; Eastimages/Getty Images, p. 22; Paul Starosta/Getty Images, p. 23; tee262/Shutterstock, p. 25; Rudi Budianto/Getty Images, p. 26; Venkata Shreeram Mallimadugula/Alamy, p. 27; Runa0410/Shutterstock, p. 28. Design elements: NikonLamp/Shutterstock; Lukasz Szwaj/Shutterstock; vi73/Shutterstock; T Studio/Shutterstock; VartB/Shutterstock.

Cover image: Jolygon/Shutterstock.